Peter Zumthor

Thinking Architecture

Peter Zumthor

Thinking Architecture

Third, expanded edition

Birkhäuser
Basel

A Way of Looking at Things

In search of the lost architecture

When I think about architecture, images come into my mind. Many of these images are connected with my training and work as an architect. They contain the professional knowledge about architecture that I have gathered over the years. Some of the other images have to do with my childhood. There was a time when I experienced architecture without thinking about it. Sometimes I can almost feel a particular door handle in my hand, a piece of metal shaped like the back of a spoon.

I used to take hold of it when I went into my aunt's garden. That door handle still seems to me like a special sign of entry into a world of different moods and smells. I remember the sound of the gravel under my feet, the soft gleam of the waxed oak staircase, I can hear the heavy front door closing behind me as I walk along the dark corridor and enter the kitchen, the only really brightly lit room in the house.

Looking back, it seems as if this was the only room in the house in which the ceiling did not disappear into twilight; the small hexagonal tiles of the floor, dark red and fitted so tightly together that the cracks between them were almost imperceptible, were hard and unyielding under my feet, and a smell of oil paint issued from the kitchen cupboard.

Everything about this kitchen was typical of a traditional kitchen. There was nothing special about it. But perhaps it was just the fact that it was so very much, so very naturally, a kitchen that has imprinted its memory indelibly on my mind. The atmosphere of this room is insolubly linked with my idea of a kitchen. Now I feel like going on and talking about the door handles that came after the handle on my aunt's garden gate, about the ground and the floors, about the soft asphalt warmed by the sun, about the flagstones covered with chestnut leaves in the autumn, and about all the doors that closed in such different ways, one replete and dignified, another with a thin, cheap clatter, others hard, implacable, and intimidating ...

Memories like these contain the deepest architectural experience that I know. They are the reservoirs of the architectural atmospheres and images that I explore in my work as an architect.

When I design a building, I frequently find myself sinking into old, half-forgotten memories, and then I try to recollect what the remembered architectural situation was really like, what it had meant to me at the time, and I try to think how it could help me now to revive that vibrant atmosphere pervaded by the simple presence of things, in which everything had its own specific place and form. And although I cannot trace any special forms, there is a hint of fullness and of richness that makes me think: this I have seen before. Yet, at the same time, I know that it is all new and different, and that there is no direct reference to a former work of architecture which might divulge the secret of the memory-laden mood.

Made of materials

To me, there is something revealing about the work of Joseph Beuys and some of the artists of the Arte Povera group. What impresses me is the precise and sensuous way they use materials. It seems anchored in an ancient, elemental knowledge about man's use of materials, and

at the same time to expose the very essence of these materials, which is beyond all culturally conveyed meaning.

I try to use materials like this in my work. I believe that they can assume a poetic quality in the context of an architectural object, although only if the architect is able to generate a meaningful situation for them, since materials in themselves are not poetic.

The sense that I try to instill into materials is beyond all rules of composition, and their tangibility, smell, and acoustic qualities are merely elements of the language that we are obliged to use. Sense emerges when I succeed in bringing out the specific meanings of certain materials in my buildings, meanings that can only be perceived in just this way in this one building.

If we work towards this goal, we must constantly ask ourselves what the use of a particular material could mean in a specific architectural context. Good answers to these questions can throw new light on both the way in which the material is generally used and its own inherent sensuous qualities.

If we succeed in this, materials in architecture can be made to shine and vibrate.

Work within things

It is said that one of the most impressive things about the music of Johann Sebastian Bach is its "architecture." Its construction seems clear and transparent. It is possible to pursue the details of the melodic, harmonic, and rhythmical elements without losing the feeling for the composition as a whole—the whole that makes sense of the details. The music seems to be based upon a clear structure, and if we trace the individual threads of the musical fabric, it is possible to apprehend the rules that govern the structure of the music.

Construction is the art of making a meaningful whole out of many parts. Buildings are witnesses to the human ability to construct concrete things. I believe that the real core of all architectural work lies in the act of construction. At the point in time when concrete materials are assembled and erected, the architecture we have been looking for becomes part of the real world.

I feel respect for the art of joining, the ability of craftsmen and engineers. I am impressed by the knowledge of how to make things, which lies at the bottom of human skill. I try to design buildings that are worthy of this knowledge and merit the challenge to this skill.

People often say "a lot of work went into this" when they sense the care and skill that its maker has lavished on a carefully constructed object. The notion that our work is an integral part of what we accomplish takes us to the very limits of our musings about the value of a work of art, a work of architecture. Are the effort and skill we put into them really inherent parts of the things we make? Sometimes, when I am moved by a work of architecture in the same way as I am moved by music, literature, or a painting, I am tempted to think so.

For the silence of sleep

I love music. The slow movements of Mozart's piano concertos, John Coltrane's ballads, or the sound of the human voice in certain songs all move me.

The human ability to invent melodies, harmonies, and rhythms amazes me.

But the world of sound also embraces the opposite of melody, harmony, and rhythm. There is disharmony and broken rhythm, fragments and clusters of sound, and there is also the purely functional sound that we call noise. Contemporary music works with these elements.

Contemporary architecture should be just as radical as contemporary music. But there are limits. Although a work of architecture based on disharmony and fragmentation, on broken rhythms, clustering and structural disruptions may be able to convey a message, as soon as we understand its statement our curiosity dies, and all that is left is the question of the building's practical usefulness.

Architecture has its own realm. It has a special physical relationship with life. I do not think of it primarily as either a message or a symbol, but as an envelope and background for life which goes on in and around it, a sensitive container for the rhythm of footsteps on the floor, for the concentration of work, for the silence of sleep.

Preliminary promises

In its final, constructed form, architecture has its place in the concrete world. This is where it exists. This is where it makes its statement. Portrayals of as yet unrealized architectural works represent an attempt to give a voice to something, which has not yet found its place in the concrete world for which it is meant.

Architectural drawings try to express as accurately as possible the aura of the building in its intended place. But precisely the effort of the portrayal often serves to underline the absence of the actual object, and what then emerges is an awareness of the inadequacy of any kind of portrayal, curiosity about the reality it promises, and perhaps—if the promise has the power to move us—a longing for its presence. If the naturalism and graphic virtuosity of architectural portrayals are too great, if they lack "open patches" where our imagination and curiosity about the reality of the drawing can penetrate the image, the portrayal itself becomes the object of our desire, and our longing for its reality wanes because there is little or nothing in the representation that points to the intended reality beyond it. The portrayal no longer holds a promise. It refers only to itself.

Design drawings that refer to a reality which still lies in the future are important in my work. I continue working on my drawings until they reach the delicate point of representation when the prevailing mood I seek emerges, and I stop before inessentials start detracting from its impact. The drawing itself must take on the quality of the sought-for object. It is like a sketch by a sculptor for his sculpture, not merely an illustration of an idea but an innate part of the work of creation, which ends with the constructed object.

These sort of drawings enable us to step back, to look, and to learn to understand that which has not yet come into being and which has just started to emerge.

Chinks in sealed objects

Buildings are artificial constructions. They consist of single parts which must be joined together. To a large degree, the quality of the finished object is determined by the quality of the joins.

In sculpture, there is a tradition that minimizes the expression of the joints and joins between the single parts in favor of the overall form. Richard Serra's steel objects, for example, look just as homogenous

and integral as the stone and wood sculptures of older sculptural traditions. Many of the installations and objects by artists of the 1960s and 70s rely on the simplest and most obvious methods of joining and connecting that we know. Beuys, Merz, and others often used loose settings in spaces, coils, folds, and layers when developing a whole from the individual parts. The direct, seemingly self-evident way in which these objects are put together is interesting. There is no interruption of the overall impression by small parts that have nothing to do with the object's statement. Our perception of the whole is not distracted by inessential details. Every touch, every join, every joint is there in order to reinforce the idea of the quiet presence of the work.

When I design buildings, I try to give them this kind of presence. However, unlike the sculptor, I have to start with functional and technical requirements that represent the fundamental task I have to fulfill. Architecture is always faced with the challenge of developing a whole out of innumerable details, out of various functions and forms, materials and dimensions. The architect must look for rational constructions and forms for edges and joints, for the points where surfaces intersect and different materials meet. These formal details determine the sensitive transitions within the larger proportions of the building. The details establish the formal rhythm, the building's finely fractionated scale. Details express what the basic idea of the design requires at the relevant point in the object: belonging or separation, tension or lightness, friction, solidity, fragility ...

Details, when they are successful, are not mere decoration. They do not distract or entertain. They lead to an understanding of the whole of which they are an inherent part.

There is a magical power in every completed, self-contained creation. It is as if we succumb to the magic of the fully developed architectural body. Our attention is caught, perhaps for the first time, by a detail such as two nails in the floor that hold the steel plates by the worn-out doorstep. Emotions well up. Something moves us.

Beyond the symbols

"Anything goes," say the doers. "Main Street is almost all right," says Venturi, the architect. "Nothing works any more," say those who suffer from the hostility of our day and age. These statements stand for contradictory opinions, if not for contradictory facts. We get used to living with contradictions and there are several reasons for this: traditions crumble, and with them cultural identities. No one seems really to understand and control the dynamics developed by economics and politics. Everything merges into everything else, and mass communication creates an artificial world of signs. Arbitrariness prevails.

Postmodern life could be described as a state in which everything beyond our own personal biography seems vague, blurred, and somehow unreal. The world is full of signs and information, which stand for things that no one fully understands because they, too, turn out to be mere signs for other things. Yet the real thing remains hidden. No one ever gets to see it. Nevertheless, I am convinced that real things do exist, however endangered they may be. There are earth and water, the light of the sun, landscapes and vegetation; and there are objects, made by man, such as machines, tools, or musical instruments, which are what they are, which are not mere vehicles for an artistic message, and whose presence is self-evident.

When we look at objects or buildings that seem to be at peace within themselves, our perception becomes calm and dulled. The objects we perceive have no message for us; they are simply there. Our perceptive faculties grow quiet, unprejudiced, and unacquisitive. They reach beyond signs and symbols; they are open, empty. It is as if we could see something on which we cannot focus our consciousness. Here, in this perceptual vacuum, a memory may surface, a memory that seems to issue from the depths of time. Now, our observation of the object embraces a presentiment of the world in all its wholeness because there is nothing that cannot be understood.

There is a power in the ordinary things of everyday life, as Edward Hopper's paintings seem to say. We only have to look at them long enough to see it.

Completed landscapes

To me, the presence of certain buildings has something secret about it. They seem simply to be there. We do not pay any special attention to them. And yet it is virtually impossible to imagine the place where they stand without them. These buildings appear to be anchored firmly in the ground. They give the impression of being a self-evident part of their surroundings and they seem to be saying: "I am as you see me and I belong here."

I have a passionate desire to design such buildings, buildings that, in time, grow naturally into being a part of the form and history of their place. Every new work of architecture intervenes in a specific historical situation. It is essential to the quality of the intervention that the new building should embrace qualities that can enter into a meaningful dialogue with the existing situation. For if the intervention is to find its place, it must make us see what already exists in a new light. We throw a stone into the water. Sand swirls up and settles again. The stir was necessary. The stone has found its place. But the pond is no longer the same.

I believe those buildings only be accepted by their surroundings if they have the ability to appeal to our emotions and minds in various ways. Since our feelings and understanding are rooted in the past, our sensuous connections with a building must respect the process of remembering.

But, as John Berger says, what we remember cannot be compared to the end of a line. Various possibilities lead to and meet in the act of remembering. Images, moods, forms, words, signs, or comparisons open up possibilities of approach. We must construct a radial system of approach that enables us to see the work of architecture as a focal point from different angles simultaneously: historically, aesthetically, functionally, personally, passionately.

The tension inside the body

Among all the drawings produced by architects, my favorites are the working drawings. Working drawings are detailed and objective. Created for the craftsmen who are to give the imagined object a material form, they are free of associative manipulation. They do not try to convince and impress like project drawings. They seem to be saying: "This is exactly how it will look."

Working drawings are like anatomical drawings. They reveal something of the secret inner tension that the finished architectural body is reluctant to divulge: the art of joining, hidden geometry, the friction of materials, the inner forces of bearing and holding, the human work that is inherent in man-made things.

Per Kirkeby once did a brick sculpture in the form of a house for a documenta exhibition in Kassel. The house had no entrance. Its interior was inaccessible and hidden. It remained a secret, which added an aura of mystical depth to the sculpture's other qualities.

I think that the hidden structures and constructions of a house should be organized in such a way that they endow the body of the building with a quality of inner tension and vibration. This is how violins are made. They remind us of the living bodies of nature.

Unexpected truths

In my youth I imagined poetry as a kind of colored cloud made up of more or less diffuse metaphors and allusions, which, although they might be enjoyable, were difficult to associate with a reliable view of the world. As an architect, I have learned to understand that the opposite of this youthful definition of poetry is probably closer to the truth.

If a work of architecture consists of forms and contents that combine to create a strong fundamental mood powerful enough to affect us, it may possess the qualities of a work of art. This art has, however, nothing to do with interesting configurations or originality. It is concerned with insights and understanding, and above all with truth. Perhaps poetry is unexpected truth. It lives in stillness. Architecture's artistic task is to give this still expectancy a form. The building itself is never poetic. At most, it may possess subtle qualities, which, at certain moments, permit us to understand something that we were never able to understand in quite this way before.

Desire

The clear, logical development of a work of architecture depends on rational and objective criteria. When I permit subjective and unconsidered ideas to intervene in the objective course of the design process, I acknowledge the significance of personal feelings in my work.

When architects talk about their buildings, what they say is often at odds with the statements of the buildings themselves. This is probably connected with the fact that they tend to talk a good deal about the rational, thought-out aspects of their work and less about the secret passion that inspires it.

The design process is based on a constant interplay of feeling and reason. The feelings, preferences, longings, and desires that emerge and demand to be given a form must be controlled by critical powers of reasoning, but it is our feelings that tell us whether abstract considerations really ring true. To a large degree, designing is based on understanding and establishing systems of order. Yet I believe that the essential substance of the architecture we seek proceeds from feeling and insight. Precious moments of intuition result from patient work. With the sudden emergence of an inner image, a new line in a drawing, the whole design changes and is newly formulated within a fraction of a second. It is as if a powerful drug were suddenly taking effect. Everything I knew before about the thing I am creating is flooded by a bright new light. I experience joy and passion, and something deep inside me seems to affirm: "I want to build this house!"

Composing in space

Geometry is about the laws of lines, plane surfaces, and three-dimensional bodies in space. Geometry can help us understand how to handle space in architecture.

In architecture, there are two basic possibilities of spatial composition: the closed architectural body that isolates space within itself, and the open body that embraces an area of space that is connected with the endless continuum. The extension of space can be made visible through bodies such as slabs or poles placed freely or in rows in the spatial expanse of a room.

I do not claim to know what space really is. The longer I think about it, the more mysterious it becomes. About one thing, however, I am sure: when we, as architects, are concerned with space, we are concerned with but a tiny part of the infinity that surrounds the earth, and yet each and every building marks a unique place in that infinity.

With this idea in mind, I start by sketching the first plans and sections of my design. I draw spatial diagrams and simple volumes. I try to visualize them as precise bodies in space, and I feel it is important to sense exactly how they define and separate an area of interior space from the space that surrounds them, or how they contain a part of the infinite spatial continuum in a kind of open vessel.

Buildings that have a strong impact always convey an intense feeling of their spatial quality. They embrace the mysterious void called space in a special way and make it vibrate.

Common sense

Designing is inventing. When I was still at arts and crafts school, we tried to follow this principle. We looked for a new solution to every problem. We felt it was important to be avant-garde. Not until later did I realize that there are basically only a very few architectural problems for which a valid solution has not already been found.

In retrospect, my education in design seems somewhat a-historical. Our role models were the pioneers and inventors of Das Neue Bauen. We regarded architectural history as part of our general education, which had little influence on our work as designers. Thus, we frequently invented what had already been invented, and we tried our hand at inventing the uninventable.

This kind of training in design is not without its educational value. Later, however, as practicing architects, we do well to get acquainted with the enormous repository of knowledge and experience contained in the history of architecture. I believe that if we integrate this in our work, we have a better chance of making a genuine contribution of our own. Architecture is, however, not a linear process that leads more or less logically and directly from architectural history to new buildings. On the search for the architecture that I envisage, I frequently experience stifling moments of emptiness. Nothing I can think of seems to tally with what I want and cannot yet envisage. At these moments, I try to shake off the academic knowledge of architecture I have acquired because it has suddenly started to hold me back. This helps. I find I can breathe more freely. I catch a whiff of the old familiar mood of the inventors and pioneers. Design has once again become invention.

The creative act in which a work of architecture comes into being goes beyond all historical and technical knowledge. Its focus is on the dialogue with the issues of our time. At the moment of its creation, architecture is bound to the present in a very special way. It reflects the spirit of its inventor and gives its own answers to the questions of our time through its functional form and appearance, its relationship with other works of architecture, and with the place where it stands.

The answers to these questions, which I can formulate as an architect, are limited. Our times of change and transition do not permit big gestures. There are only a few remaining common values left upon which we can build and which we all share. I thus appeal for a kind of architecture of common sense based on the fundamentals that we still know, understand, and feel. I carefully observe the concrete appearance of the world, and in my buildings I try to enhance what seems to be valuable, to correct what is disturbing, and to create anew what we feel is missing.

Melancholy perceptions

Ettore Scola's film Le Bal recounts fifty years of European history with no dialogue and a complete unity of place. It consists solely of music and the motion of people moving and dancing. We remain in the same room with the same people throughout, while time goes by and the dancers grow older.

The focus of the film is on its main characters. But it is the ballroom with its tiled floor and its paneling, the stairs in the background, and the lion's paw at the side that creates the film's dense, powerful atmosphere. Or is it the other way around? Is it the people who endow the room with its particular mood?

I ask this question because I am convinced that a good building must be capable of absorbing the traces of human life and thus of taking on a specific richness.

Naturally, in this context I think of the patina of age on materials, of innumerable small scratches on surfaces, of varnish that has grown dull and brittle, and of edges polished by use. But when I close my eyes and try to forget both these physical traces and my own first associations,

what remains is a different impression, a deeper feeling—a consciousness of time passing and an awareness of the human lives that have
been acted out in these places and rooms and charged them with a
special aura. At these moments, architecture's aesthetic and practical
values, stylistic and historical significance are of secondary importance.
What matters now is only this feeling of deep melancholy. Architecture is exposed to life. If its body is sensitive enough, it can assume a
quality that bears witness to the reality of past life.

Steps left behind

When I work on a design I allow myself to be guided by images and
moods that I remember and can relate to the kind of architecture I am
looking for. Most of the images that come to mind originate from my
subjective experience and are only rarely accompanied by a remembered architectural commentary. While I am designing I try to find out
what these images mean so that I can learn how to create a wealth of
visual forms and atmospheres.

After a certain time, the object I am designing takes on some of the
qualities of the images I use as models. If I can find a meaningful way of
interlocking and superimposing these qualities, the object will assume a
depth and richness. If I am to achieve this effect, the qualities I am giving
the design must merge and blend with the constructional and formal
structure of the finished building. Form and construction, appearance
and function are no longer separate. They belong together and form
a whole.

When we look at the finished building, our eyes, guided by our ana-
lytical mind, tend to stray and look for details to hold on to. But the

synthesis of the whole does not become comprehensible through isolated details. Everything refers to everything.

At this moment, the initial images fade into the background. The models, words, and comparisons that were necessary for the creation of the whole disappear like steps that have been left behind. The new building assumes the focal position and is itself. Its history begins.

Resistance

I believe that architecture today needs to reflect on the tasks and possibilities which are inherently its own. Architecture is not a vehicle or a symbol for things that do not belong to its essence. In a society that celebrates the inessential, architecture can put up a resistance, counteract the waste of forms and meanings, and speak its own language.

I believe that the language of architecture is not a question of a specific style. Every building is built for a specific use in a specific place and for a specific society. My buildings try to answer the questions that emerge from these simple facts as precisely and critically as they can.

The Hard Core of Beauty

Two weeks ago I happened to hear a radio program on the American poet William Carlos Williams. The program was entitled *The Hard Core of Beauty*. This phrase caught my attention. I like the idea that beauty has a hard core, and when I think of architecture this association of beauty and a hard core has a certain familiarity. "The machine is a thing that has no superfluous parts," Williams is supposed to have said. And I immediately think I know what he meant. It's a thought that Peter Handke alludes to, I feel, when he says that beauty lies in natural, grown things that do not carry any signs or messages, and when he adds that he is upset when he cannot discover the meaning of things for himself.

And then I learned from the radio program that the poetry of William Carlos Williams is based on the conviction that there are no ideas except in the things themselves, and that the purpose of his art was to direct his sensory perception to the world of things in order to make them his own.

In Williams's work, said the speaker, this takes place seemingly unemotionally and laconically, and it is precisely for this reason that his texts have such a strong emotional impact.

What I heard appeals to me: not to wish to stir up emotions with buildings, I think to myself, but to allow emotions to emerge, to be. And: to remain close to the thing itself, close to the essence of the thing I have to shape, confident that if the building is conceived accurately enough for its place and its function, it will develop its own strength, with no need for artistic additions. The hard core of beauty: concentrated substance.

But where are architecture's fields of force that constitute its substance, above and beyond all superficiality and arbitrariness?

Italo Calvino tells us in his *Lezioni americane* about the Italian poet Giacomo Leopardi who saw the beauty of a work of art, in his case the beauty of literature, in its vagueness, openness, and indeterminacy, because this leaves the form open for many different meanings.

Leopardi's observation seems convincing enough. Works or objects of art that move us are multifaceted; they have numerous and perhaps endless layers of meaning that overlap and interweave, and that change as we change our angle of observation.

But how is the architect to obtain this depth and multiplicity in a building of his making? Can vagueness and openness be planned? Is there not a contradiction here to the claim of accuracy that Williams's argument seems to imply?

Calvino finds a surprising answer to this in a text by Leopardi. Calvino points out that in Leopardi's own texts, this lover of the indeterminate reveals a painstaking fidelity to the things he describes and offers to our contemplation, and he comes to the conclusion: "This, then, is what Leopardi demands of us so that we can enjoy the beauty of the indeterminate and vague! He calls for highly accurate and pedantic attention in the composition of each picture, in the meticulous definition of details, in the choice of objects, lighting, and atmosphere with the aim of attaining the desired vagueness." Calvino closes with the seemingly paradoxical proclamation: "The poet of the vague can only be the poet of precision!"

What interests me in this story reported by Calvino is not the exhortation to precision and patient, detailed work with which we are all familiar, but the implication that richness and multiplicity emanate from the things themselves if we observe them attentively and give them their due. Applied to architecture, this means for me that power and multiplicity must be developed from the assigned task or, in other words, from the things that constitute it.

John Cage said in one of his lectures that he is not a composer who hears music in his mind and then attempts to write it down. He has another way of operating. He works out concepts and structures and then has them performed to find out how they sound.

When I read this statement I remembered how we recently developed a project for a thermal bath in the mountains in my studio, not by forming preliminary images of the building in our minds and subsequently adapting them to the assignment, but by endeavoring to answer basic questions arising from the location of the given site, the purpose, and the building materials—mountain, rock, water—which at first had no visual content in terms of existing architecture.

It was only after we had succeeded in answering, step by step, the questions posed by the site, purpose, and material that structures and spaces emerged which surprised us and which I believe possess the potential of a primordial force that reaches deeper than the mere arrangement of stylistically preconceived forms.

Occupying oneself with the inherent laws of concrete things such as mountains, rock, and water in connection with a building assignment offers a chance of apprehending and expressing some of the primal and as it were "culturally innocent" attributes of these elements, and of developing an architecture that sets out from and returns to real things. Preconceived images and stylistically pre-fabricated formal idioms are qualified only to block access to this goal.

My Swiss colleagues Herzog and de Meuron say that architecture as a single whole no longer exists today, and that it accordingly has to be artificially created in the head of the designer, as an act of precise thinking. The two architects derive from this assumption their theory of architecture as a form of thought, an architecture that, I suppose, should reflect its cerebrally conceived wholeness in a special way.

I do not intend to pursue these architects' theory of architecture as a form of thought, but only the assumption on which it is based, namely that the wholeness of a building in the old sense of the master builders no longer exists.

Personally, I still believe in the self-sufficient, corporeal wholeness of an architectural object as the essential, if difficult, aim of my work, if not as a natural or given fact.

Yet how are we to achieve this wholeness in architecture at a time when the divine, which once gave things a meaning, and even reality itself seem to be dissolving in the endless flux of transitory signs and images?

Peter Handke writes of his endeavors to make texts and descriptions part of the environment they relate to. If I understand him correctly, I am confronted here not only by the all-too-familiar awareness of the difficulty of eliminating artificiality in things created in an artificial act and of making them part of the world of ordinary and natural things, but also by the belief that truth lies in the things themselves.

I believe that if artistic processes strive for wholeness, they always attempt to give their creations a presence akin to that found in the things of nature or in the natural environment. Consequently, I find that I can understand Handke, who in the same interview refers to himself as a writer about places, when he requires of his texts that "there should be no additives in them, but a cognizance of details and of their interlinking to form a factual complex."

The word Handke uses to designate what I have here called a factual complex, namely *Sachverhalt*, seems to me to be meaningful with regard to the aim of whole and unadulterated things: exact factual contents must be brought together, buildings must be thought of as complexes whose details have been rightly identified and put into a factual relationship to each other. A factual relationship!

The point that emerges here is the reduction of the contents to real things. Handke also speaks, in this context, of fidelity to things. He would like his descriptions, he says, to be experienced as faithfulness to the place they describe and not as supplementary coloring.

Statements of this kind help me to come to terms with the dissatisfaction I often experience when I contemplate recent architecture. I frequently come across buildings that have been designed with a good deal of effort and a will to find a special form, and I find I am put off by them. The architect responsible for the building is not present, but he talks to me unceasingly from every detail, he keeps on saying the same thing, and I quickly lose interest. Good architecture should receive the human visitor, should enable him to experience it and live in it, but it should not constantly talk at him.

Why, I often wonder, is the obvious but difficult solution so rarely tried? Why do we have so little confidence in the basic things architecture is made from: material, structure, construction, bearing and being borne, earth and sky, and confidence in spaces that are really allowed to be spaces—spaces whose enclosing walls and constituent materials, concavity, emptiness, light, air, odor, receptivity, and resonance are handled with respect and care?

I personally like the idea of designing and building houses from which I can withdraw at the end of the forming process, leaving behind a building that is itself, that serves as a place to live in and a part of the world of things, and that can manage perfectly well without my personal rhetoric.

To me, buildings can have a beautiful silence that I associate with attributes such as composure, self-evidence, durability, presence, and integrity, and with warmth and sensuousness as well; a building that is being itself, being a building, not representing anything, just being.

Say that it is a crude effect, black reds,
Pink yellows, orange whites, too much as they are
To be anything else in the sunlight of the room.
Too much as they are to be changed by metaphor,
Too actual, things that in being real
Make any imaginings of them lesser things.

This is the beginning of the poem *Bouquet of Roses in Sunlight* by the American poet of quiet contemplation, Wallace Stevens.

Wallace Stevens, I read in the introduction to his collection of poems, accepted the challenge of looking long, patiently, and exactly and of dis-covering and understanding things. His poems are not a protest or a complaint against a lost law and order, nor are they the expression

of any sort of consternation, but they seek a harmony which is possible all the same and which—in his case—can only be that of the poem. (Calvino goes a step further along this line of thought in an attempt to define his literary work when he says that he has only one defense against the loss of form that he sees all around him: an idea of literature.) Reality was the goal to which Stevens aspired. Surrealism, it appears, did not impress him, for it invents without discovering. He pointed out that to portray a shell playing an accordion is to invent, not discover. And so it crops up once again, this fundamental thought that I seem to find in Williams and Handke, and that I also sense in the paintings of Edward Hopper: it is only between the reality of things and the imagination that the spark of the work of art is kindled.

If I translate this statement into architectural terms, I tell myself that the spark of the successful building can only be kindled between the reality of the things pertaining to it and the imagination. And this is no revelation to me, but the confirmation of something I continually strive for in my work, and the confirmation of a wish whose roots seem to be deep inside me.

But to return to the question one final time: where do I find the reality on which I must concentrate my powers of imagination when attempting to design a building for a particular place and purpose?

One key to the answer lies, I believe, in the words "place" and "purpose" themselves.

In an essay entitled "Building Dwelling Thinking," Martin Heidegger wrote: "Living among things is the basic principle of human existence," which I understand to mean that we are never in an abstract world but always in a world of things, even when we think. And, once again

Heidegger: "The relationship of man to places and through places to spaces is based on his dwelling in them."

The concept of dwelling, understood in Heidegger's wide sense of living and thinking in places and spaces, contains an exact reference to what reality means to me as an architect.

It is not the reality of theories detached from things, it is the reality of the concrete building assignment relating to the act or state of dwelling that interests me and upon which I wish to concentrate my imaginative faculties. It is the reality of building materials, stone, cloth, steel, leather …, and the reality of the structures I use to construct the building whose properties I wish to penetrate with my imagination, bringing meaning and sensuousness to bear so that the spark of the successful building may be kindled, a building that can serve as a home for man.

The reality of architecture is the concrete body in which forms, volumes, and spaces come into being. There are no ideas except in things.

From a Passion for Things to the Things Themselves

It is important to me to reflect about architecture, to step back from my daily work and take a look at what I am doing and why I am doing it. I love doing this, and I think I need it, too. I do not work towards architecture from a theoretically defined point of departure, for I am committed to making architecture, to building, to an ideal of perfection, just as in my boyhood I used to make things according to my ideas, things that had to be just right, for reasons which I do not really understand. It was always there, this deeply personal feeling for the things I made for myself, and I never thought of it as being anything special. It was just there.

Today, I am aware that my work as an architect is largely a quest for this early passion, this obsession, and an attempt to understand it better and to refine it. And when I reflect on whether I have since added new images and passions to the old ones, and whether I have learned something in my training and practice, I realize that in some way I seem always to have known the intuitive core of new discoveries.

Places

I live and work in Graubünden, in a farming village surrounded by mountains. I sometimes wonder whether this has influenced my work, and the thought that it probably has is not unpleasant.

Would the buildings I design look different if, instead of living in Graubünden, I had spent the past twenty-five years in the landscape of my youth on the northern foothills of the Jura mountains, with their

rolling hills and beech woods and the familiar, reassuring vicinity of the urbane city of Basel?

As soon as I begin to think about this question, I realize that my work has been influenced by many places.

When I concentrate on a specific site or place for which I am going to design a building, when I try to plumb its depths, its form, its history, and its sensuous qualities, images of other places start to invade this process of precise observation: images of places that I know and that once impressed me, images of ordinary or special places that I carry with me as inner visions of specific moods and qualities; images of architectural situations, which emanate from the world of art, of films, theater, or literature.

Sometimes they come to me unbidden, these images of places that are frequently at first glance inappropriate or alien, images of places of many different origins. At other times I summon them. I need them, for it is only when I confront and compare the essentials of different places, when I allow similar, related, or maybe alien elements to cast their light on the place of my intervention that the focused, multi-faceted image of the local essence of the site emerges, a vision that reveals connections, exposes lines of force, and creates excitement. It is now that the fertile, creative ground appears, and the network of possible approaches to the specific place emerges and triggers the processes and decisions of design. So I immerse myself in the place and try to inhabit it in my imagination, and at the same time I look beyond it at the world of my other places.

When I come across a building that has developed a special presence in connection with the place it stands in, I sometimes feel that it is imbued with an inner tension that refers to something over and above the place itself.

It seems to be part of the essence of its place, and at the same time it speaks of the world as a whole.

When an architectural design draws solely from tradition and only repeats the dictates of its site, I sense a lack of a genuine concern with the world and the emanations of contemporary life. If a work of architecture speaks only of contemporary trends and sophisticated visions without triggering vibrations in its place, this work is not anchored in its site, and I miss the specific gravity of the ground it stands on.

Observations

1 We were standing around the drawing table talking about a project by an architect whom we all hold in high regard. I considered the project interesting in many ways. I mentioned several of its specific qualities and added that some time previously I had laid aside my positive prejudice, which sprang from my high estimation of the architect, and taken an unbiased look at the project. And I had come to the conclusion that, as a whole, I did not really like it. We discussed the possible reasons for my impression and came up with a few details without arriving at a valid conclusion. And then one of the younger members of the group, a talented and usually rationally minded architect, said: "It is an interesting building for all sorts of theoretical and practical reasons. The trouble is, it has no soul."

Some weeks later, I was sitting outdoors drinking coffee with my wife and discussing the issue of buildings with a soul. We talked about several works of architecture that we knew, and described them to each other. And when we recalled buildings that had the characteristics we were looking for and pinpointed their special qualities, we became aware that there are buildings that we love. And whereas we knew almost at once which ones belonged to the special category in which we were interested, we found it difficult to find a common denominator for their qualities. Our attempt to generalize seemed to rob the individual buildings of their splendor.

But the subject continued to prey on my mind, and I resolved to try and write some brief descriptions of architectural situations that I love, fragmentary approaches based on personal experiences that have a connection with my work, and in so doing to move within the same mental framework in which I think when I am concerned with generating the essentials of a work of my own.

2 The main rooms of the small mountain hotel overlooked the valley on the broad side of the long building. It had two adjacent wood-paneled reception rooms on the ground floor, both of them accessible from the corridor and connected by a door. The smaller of them looked like a comfortable place in which to sit and read, and the larger one, with five well-placed tables, was clearly the place in which meals were served. On the first-floor there were bedrooms with deep, shady wooden balconies, on the second floor more bedrooms opening onto terraces.

I would enjoy looking at the open sky from the upper rooms, I thought, as we approached the hotel for the first time. But the thought of staying in one of the first-floor rooms and reading or writing in the intimate atmosphere of the shady balcony in the late afternoon in turn seemed no less inviting.

There was an opening in the wall at the foot of the staircase leading from the upper floors to the entrance. A serving hatch. In the early afternoons it held fruit flans on white plates for the guests. The smell of the fresh flans took us by surprise as we came down the stairs, and kitchen noises issued from the half-open door of the opposite room.

After a day or two we knew our way around. There were deck chairs stacked along the side of the hotel, which adjoins the meadow. A little way away, in the half shadow at the edge of the wood, we noticed a woman sitting in a deck chair, reading. We picked up two of the chairs and looked for a spot of our own. During the day we usually drank our coffee at one of the wooden folding tables on the narrow veranda at the front. They were hinged at regular intervals along the front parapet. Good places to sit, these small tables clinging to the edge of the veranda; the sill was just the right height for use as an elbow rest.

Conversations with the other guests usually took place at dusk at the other veranda tables, placed in a row against the façade and protected from the weather by the projecting upper floors. The French window to the veranda was opened after the evening meal; we all stretched our legs and looked out over the valley, and then sat with a drink by the wall that was still warm from the day's sunshine. Once, after the evening meal, we were invited to sit at the large corner table at the far end of the veranda near the entrance. During the day, that spot always seemed to be used by the regulars of the house. I never sat in this niche, which caught the morning sun at the other end of the veranda. On sunny mornings there was usually someone already sitting there, reading.

When I think about buildings that provide me with natural spatial conditions appropriate to the place, to the daily routine, my activities and the way I am feeling, when I conjure up mental pictures of works of architecture that give me space to live and seem to anticipate and satisfy my needs, this mountain hotel always comes to mind. It was designed by a painter for himself and his guests.

3 Our first impression of the outside of the restaurant made us hopeful that we had found something better than the other places along the main road of the tourist village. We were not disappointed. Entering through the narrow porch, which, as it turned out, was built from the inside behind the main door like a wooden shed, we found ourselves in a large, high-ceilinged, hall-like room, its walls and ceiling lined with dark, mat, gleaming wood: regularly placed frames and panels, wainscoting, cornices, indented joists resting on brackets with ornamental scrolls.

The atmosphere of the room seemed dark, even gloomy, until our eyes grew accustomed to the light. The gloom soon gave way to a mood of gentleness. The daylight entering through the tall, rhythmically placed windows lit up certain sections of the room, while other parts, which did not benefit from the reflection of the light from the paneling, lay withdrawn in half-shadow.

As soon as I entered the room my eye was caught by an extension in the center of the long outer wall, a semi-circular bulge large enough to accommodate five tables along the curved wall by the windows. The floor of the room-height niche was on a slightly higher level than the rest of the hall. No doubt about it, I thought, this was where I wanted to sit. Two of the tables were still free. The people sitting there, doubtless ordinary guests of the restaurant, had a privileged air about them.

We hesitated and finally decided on a table in the almost empty main part of the hall. Yet we hesitated again, and instead of sitting down we went in search of service. After a while a girl appeared through a door in the paneling of the inner wall and led us to a table in the niche. We sat down. The slight feeling of irritation occasioned by our arrival soon abated. We lit our first cigarettes and ordered some wine.

At the next table two women were holding an animated conversation. One of them was speaking American, the other Swiss German. Neither of them spoke a word in the other's language. The voices of the people in the group at the next table but one sounded pleasantly far away. I looked around and gradually absorbed the mood. I felt at ease sitting in the light of one of the windows, which now seemed taller than ever, and looking into the darkened expanse of the hall. The other guests, busy with their conversations and their meals, also seemed happy to be sitting there; they behaved naturally, undisturbed by other people's presence, with an unconstrained considerateness for their fellow guests, which lent them an air of dignity. Occupied as I was with my own activities, my gaze nevertheless alighted occasionally on other faces, and I realized that I liked the feeling of their proximity—in this room in which we all looked our best.

4 Driving along a road on the coast of California, we finally arrived at the school that was listed in the architectural guide: a sprawling complex of pavilions spread out over a large expanse of flat land high over the Pacific. Barely any trees, karstic rock thrusting through the turf, a few houses in the immediate vicinity. The rows of tall, single-story buildings with flat, projecting roofs were connected by asphalt paths covered by concrete slabs on steel columns, and the regular arrangement of the paths and pavilions which appeared to accommodate the classrooms was periodically interrupted by buildings with a special function at which we could only guess. It was during the school holidays and the complex was deserted. The windows were set high up in the walls and it was hard to see into the classrooms. We came across a large metal door to a side courtyard, which seemed to belong to one of the classrooms. It was slightly open, and we managed to catch a glimpse of a room with desks and a blackboard. It was plainly furnished. The walls and the floor showed signs of intensive use, and the daylight entering through the high windows lent the room an atmosphere that was both concentrated and gentle.

Protection from the sun, shelter from the wind and rain, an intelligent approach to the issue of lighting, I thought, and I was aware that I had by no means grasped all the specific qualities of this architecture—the straightforward simplicity of its structure, for example, which was reminiscent of industrial precast concrete constructions, or its spaciousness, or its lack of the pedantic refinements that abound in schools in Switzerland.

My visit had been worthwhile. Once again, I resolved to begin my work with the simple, practical things, to make these things big and good and beautiful, to make them the starting point of the specific form, like a master builder who understands his métier.

5 At the age of eighteen, when I was approaching the end of my apprenticeship as a cabinetmaker, I made my first self-designed pieces of furniture. The master cabinetmaker or the client determined the form of

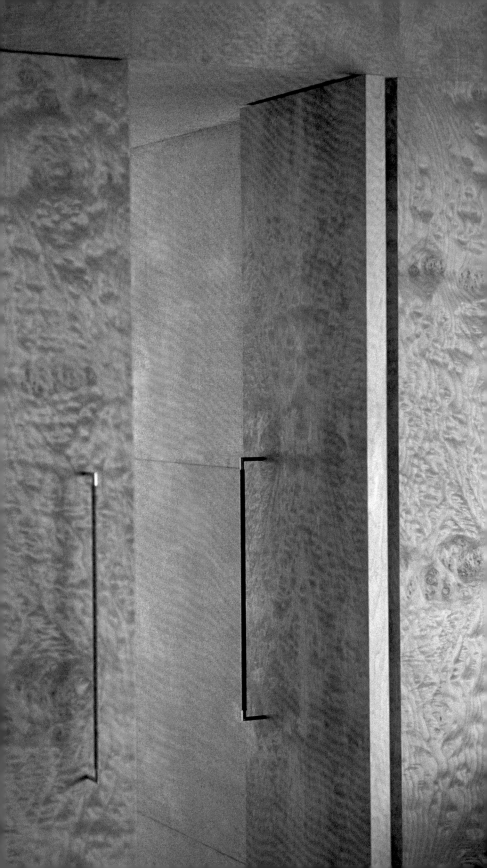

most of the furniture made in our shop, and I seldom liked it. I did not even like the wood we used for the best pieces: walnut. I chose light-colored ash for my bed and cupboard, and I made them so that they looked good on all sides, with the same wood and the same careful work back and front. I disregarded the usual practice of expending less time and care on the back because no one ever sees it anyway. At long last I was able to round off the edges only slightly without being corrected, running the sandpaper swiftly and lightly over the edges to soften their sharpness without losing the elegance and fineness of the lines. I barely touched the corners where three edges meet. I fitted the door of the cupboard into the frame at the front with a maximum of precision so that it closed almost hermetically, with a gentle frictional resistance and a barely audible sound of escaping air.

I felt good working on this cupboard. Making the precisely fitting joints and exact shapes to form a whole, a complete object that corresponded to my inner vision, triggered in me a state of intense concentration, and the finished piece of furniture added a freshness to my environment.

6 The idea is the following: a long, narrow block of basalt stone projecting a good three stories out of the ground. The block is hollowed out on all sides until only a long middle rib and a number of transverse, horizontal ribs remain. Seen in cross-section, the imagined block now looks like a geometrical tree or the letter T with three horizontal strokes: a stone object on the outskirts of the Old Town, dark, almost black, mat, gleaming—and at the same time the load bearing and spatial structure of a three-story building—cast in dark stained cement, jointless, varnished with stone oil, with surfaces that feel like paraffin wax. Door-sized openings in the ribs, simple holes in the stone, expose the sheer mass of the material. We handle this stone sculpture with the utmost care, for even at this stage it is already almost the whole building. We design the joints of the boards in which it is cast like a fine network covering all the surfaces with a regular pattern, and we are careful to ensure that the joints arising during the section-wise casting of the concrete will disappear into the network. The thin steel frames projecting from the stone like blades in the middle of the door are intended to hold the wings of the doors, and lightweight glass and sheet metal panels are inserted between the stone consoles of the floor slabs so that the intermediate spaces between the ribs become rooms like glazed verandas.

Our clients are of the opinion that the careful way in which we treat our materials, the way we develop the joints and transitions from one element of the building to the other, and the precision of detail to which we aspire are all too elaborate. They want us to use more common components and constructions, they do not want us to make such high demands on the craftsmen and technicians who are collaborating with us: they want us to build more cheaply.

When I think of the air of quality that the building could eventually emanate on its appointed site in five years or five decades, when I consider that to the people who will encounter it, the only thing that will count is what they see, that which was finally constructed, I do not find it so hard to put up a resistance to our clients' wishes.

7 I revisited the hall with the niche in the end wall that I liked so much and which I tried to describe earlier. I was no longer sure whether the floor of the niche was really on a higher level than the rest of the hall. It was not. Nor was the difference in brightness between the niche and the hall as great as I remembered it, and I was disappointed by the dull light on the wall paneling.

This difference between the reality and my memories did not surprise me. I have never been a good observer, and I have never really wanted to be. I like absorbing moods, moving in spatial situations, and I am satisfied when I am able to retain a feeling, a strong general impression from which I can later extract details as from a painting, and when I can wonder what it was that triggered the sense of protection, warmth, lightness, or spaciousness that has stayed in my memory. When I look back like this it seems impossible to distinguish between architecture and life, between spatial situations and the way I experience them. Even when I concentrate exclusively on the architecture and try to understand what I have seen, my perception of it resonates in what I have experienced and thus colors what I have observed. Memories of similar experiences thrust their way in, too, and thus images of related architectural situations overlap. The difference in the floor levels of the niche and the hall could well have existed. Perhaps it even did exist once and was later removed? Or, if it was never there, perhaps it should be added, as an improvement to the room?

Now I have fallen back into my role as an architect, and I realize once more how much I enjoy working with my old passions and images, and how they help me to find what I am looking for.

The Body of Architecture

Observations, impressions

1 I was interviewed by the curator of the museum. He tried to sound me out by means of clever, unexpected questions. What did I think about architecture, what was important to me about my work—these were the things he wanted to know. The tape recorder was on. I did my best. At the end of the interview, I realized that I was not really satisfied with my answers.

Later that evening, I talked to a friend about Aki Kaurismäki's latest film. I admire the director's empathy and respect for his characters. He does not keep his actors on a leash; he does not exploit them to express a concept, but rather shows them in a light that lets us sense their dignity, and their secrets. Kaurismäki's art lends his films a feeling of warmth, I told my colleague—and then I knew what it was I would have liked to have said on the tape this morning. To build houses like Kaurismäki makes films—that's what I would like to do.

2 The hotel in which I was staying was remodeled by a French star designer whose work I do not know because I am not interested in trendy design. But from the moment I entered the hotel, the atmosphere created by his architecture began to take effect. Artificial light illuminated the hall like a stage. Abundant muted light. Bright accents on the reception desks, different kinds of natural stone in niches in the wall. People ascending the graceful stairway to the encircling gallery stood out against a shining golden wall. Above, one could sit in one of

the dress circle boxes overlooking the hall and have a drink or a snack. There are only good seats here. Christopher Alexander, who speaks in *Pattern Language* of spatial situations in which people instinctively feel good, would have been pleased. I sat in a box overlooking the hall, a spectator, feeling that I was part of the designer's stage set. I liked looking down on the activity below where people came and went, entered and exited. I felt I understood why the architect is so successful.

3 She had seen a small house by Frank Lloyd Wright that made a great impression on her, said H. Its rooms were so small and intimate, the ceilings so low. There was a tiny library with special lighting and a lot of decorative architectural elements, and the whole house made a strong horizontal impression which she had never experienced before. The old lady was still living there. There was no need for me to go and see the house, I thought. I knew just what she meant, and I knew the feeling of "home" that she described.

4 The members of the jury were shown buildings by architects competing for an architectural award. I studied the documents describing a small red house in a rural setting, a barn converted into a dwelling which had been enlarged by the architect and the inhabitants. The extension was a success, I thought. Although you could see what had been done to the house beneath the saddle roof, the change was well modeled and integrated. The window openings were sensitively placed. The old and the new were balanced and harmonious. The new parts of the house did not seem to be saying "I am new," but rather "I am part of the new whole." Nothing spectacular or innovative, nothing striking. Based per-

haps on a somewhat outdated design principle, an old-fashioned approach attuned to craftsmanship. We agreed that we could not award this conversion a prize for design—for that, its architectural claims were too modest. Yet I enjoy thinking back on the small red house.

5 In a book about timber construction, my attention was caught by photographs of huge areas of closely packed tree trunks floating on wide expanses of water. I also liked the picture on the cover of the book, a collage of lengths of wood arranged in layers like a cross section. The numerous photos of wooden buildings, despite the fact that they were architecturally commendable, were less appealing. I have not built wooden houses for a long time.

A young colleague asked me how I would go about building a house of wood after working for some years with stone and concrete, steel and glass. At once, I had a mental image of a house-sized block of solid timber, a dense volume made of the biological substance of wood, horizontally layered and precisely hollowed out. A house like this would change its shape, would swell and contract, expand and decrease in height, a phenomenon that would have to be an integral part of the design. My young colleague told me that in Spanish, his mother tongue, the words wood, mother, and material were similar: *madera, madre, materia*. We started talking about the sensuous qualities and cultural significance of the elemental materials of wood and stone, and about how we could express these in our buildings.

6 Central Park South, New York, a hall on the first floor. It was evening. Before me, framed by the soaring, shining, stony city, lay the huge wooded rectangle of the park. Great cities are based on great, clear, well-ordered concepts, I thought. The rectangular pattern of the streets, the diagonal line of Broadway, the coastal lines of the peninsula. The buildings, packed densely in their right-angled grid, looming up in the sky, individualistic, in love with themselves, anonymous, reckless, tamed by the straitjacket of the grid.

7 The former townhouse looked somewhat lost in the park-like expanse. It was the only building in that part of the town to have survived the destruction of the Second World War. Previously used as an embassy, it was now being enlarged by a third of its original size according to the plans of a competent architect. Hard and self-assured, the extension stood side by side with the old building: on the one hand a hewn stone base, stucco façades, and balustrades, on the other a compressed modern annex made of exposed concrete, a restrained, disciplined volume that alluded to the old main building while maintaining a distinct, dialogic distance in terms of its design.

I found myself thinking about the old castle in my village. It has been altered and extended many times over the centuries, developing gradually from a cluster of free-standing buildings into a closed complex with an inner courtyard. A new architectural whole emerged at each stage of its development. Historical incongruities were not architecturally recorded. The old was adapted to the new, or the new to the old, in the interest of the complete, integrated appearance of its latest stage of evolution. Only when one analyzes the substance of the walls, strips them of their plaster, and examines their joints do these old buildings reveal their complex genesis.

8 I entered the exhibition pavilion. Once again, I was confronted by sloping walls, slanted planes, surfaces linked loosely and playfully together, battens and ropes hanging, leaning, floating, or pulling, taut or projecting. The composition disclaimed the right angle and sought an informal balance. The architecture made a dynamic impression, symbolizing movement. Its gestures filled the available space, wanting to be looked at, to make their mark. There was hardly any room left for me. I followed the winding path indicated by the architecture.

In the next pavilion I met with the spacious elegance of the Brazilian master Niemeyer's sweeping lines and forms. Once again, my interest was captured by the large rooms and the emptiness of the huge outdoor spaces in the photos of his work.

9 A. told me she had seen many tattooed women on the beach of a small seaside resort in the Cinque Terre region, a holiday destination visited mainly by Italians. The women underline the individuality of their bodies, use them to proclaim their identity. The body as a refuge in a world which would appear to be flooded by artificial signs of life, and in which philosophers ponder on virtual reality.

The human body as an object of contemporary art. Surveys, disclosures that seek knowledge, or the human body as a fetish of self-assertion that can only succeed when looked at in the mirror or seen through the eyes of others?

This autumn I visited the room with the exhibition of contemporary architectural projects from France. I saw shining objects made of glass, gentle shapes without edges. Taut, elegant curves rounding off the geometrical volumes of the objects at specific points. Their lines

reminded me of Rodin's drawings of nudes and endowed the objects with the quality of sculptures. Architectural models. Models. Beautiful bodies, celebrations of surface texture, skin, hermetic and flawless, embracing the bodies.

10 A glass partition divided up the length of the narrow corridor of the old hotel. The wing of a door below, a firmly fixed pane of glass above, no frame, the panes clamped and held at the corners by two metal clasps. Normally done, nothing special. Certainly not a design by an architect. But I liked the door. Was it because of the proportions of the two panes of glass, the form and position of the clamps, the gleaming of the glass in the muted colors of the dark corridor, or was it because the upper pane of glass, which was taller than the average-height swing door below it, emphasized the height of the corridor? I did not know.

11 I was shown some photographs of a complicated building. Different areas, planes, and volumes seemed to overlap, slanting and erect, encapsulated one within the other. The building, whose unusual appearance gave me no clear indication as to its function, made a strangely overloaded and tortured impression. Somehow, it seemed two-dimensional. For I moment I thought I was looking at a photograph of a cardboard model, colorfully painted. Later, when I learned the name of the architect, I was shocked. Had I made a mistake, a premature, ignorant judgment? The architect's name has an international ring, his fine architectural drawings are well known, and his written statements about contemporary architecture, which also deal with philosophical themes, are widely published.

12 A town house in Manhattan with a good address, just completed. The new façade in the line of the street of buildings stood out distinctly. In the photographs, the natural stone shield, surrounded by glass, looked like a backdrop. In reality, the façade was more uniform, more integrated in its surroundings. My instinct to criticize vanished when I entered the house. The quality of its construction captured my attention. The architect received us, took us into the vestibule, and showed us from room to room. The rooms were spacious, their order logical. We were eager to see each succeeding room, and we were not disappointed. The quality of the daylight entering through the glazed rear façade and a skylight over the stairs was pleasant. On all the floors, the presence of the intimate backyard around which the main rooms were grouped was perceptible, even at the heart of the building.

The architect spoke in respectful, amicable terms of the clients, the newly installed residents, of their understanding of his work, of his efforts to comply with their requirements, and of their criticism of some impractical aspects which he subsequently improved. He opened cupboard doors, lowered the large scrim blinds, which suffused the living room with a mellow light, showed us folding partitions, and demonstrated huge swing doors that moved noiselessly between two pivots, closing tightly and precisely. Every now and then, he touched the surface of some material or ran his hands over a handrail, a joint in the wood, the edge of a glass pane.

13 The town I was visiting had a particularly attractive neighborhood. Buildings from the 19th century and the turn of the century, solid volumes placed along the streets and squares, constructed of stone and brick. Nothing exceptional. Typically urban. The public premises on the lower floors faced the road, the dwellings and offices above retreated behind protective façades, hiding private spheres behind prestigious faces, anonymous faces, clearly divorced from the public space, which began with a hard edge at the foot of the façades.

I had been told that a number of architects lived and worked in this neighborhood. I remembered this a few days later when I was looking at a new neighborhood nearby, designed by well-known architects, and I found myself thinking about the unequivocal backs and fronts of the urban structures, the precisely articulated public spaces, the graciously restrained façades and exactly fitting volumes for the body of the town.

14 We spent years developing the concept, the form, and the working drawings of our stone-built thermal baths. Then construction began. I was standing in front of one of the first blocks that the masons had built in stone from a nearby quarry. I was surprised and irritated. Although everything corresponded exactly with our plans, I had not expected this concurrent hardness and softness, this smooth yet rugged quality, this iridescent gray-green presence emanating from the square stone blocks. For a moment, I had the feeling that our project had escaped us and become independent because it had evolved into a material entity that obeyed its own laws.

15 I visited an exhibition of work by Meret Oppenheim at the Guggenheim Museum. The techniques she uses are strikingly varied. There is no continuous, consistent style. Nevertheless, I experienced her way of thinking, her way of looking at the world and of intervening in it through her work, as coherent and integral. So there is probably no

point in wondering just what it is that stylistically links the famous fur cup and the snake made up of pieces of coal. Didn't Meret Oppenheim once say that every idea needs its proper form to be effective?

Teaching Architecture, Learning Architecture

Young people go to university with the aim of becoming architects, of finding out if they have got what it takes. What is the first thing we should teach them?

First of all, we must explain that the person standing in front of them is not someone who asks questions whose answers he already knows. Practicing architecture is asking oneself questions, finding one's own answers with the help of the teacher, whittling down, finding solutions. Over and over again.

The strength of a good design lies in ourselves and in our ability to perceive the world with both emotion and reason. A good architectural design is sensuous. A good architectural design is intelligent.

We all experience architecture before we have even heard the word. The roots of architectural understanding lie in our architectural experience: our room, our house, our street, our village, our town, our landscape—we experience them all early on, unconsciously, and we subsequently compare them with the countryside, towns, and houses that we experience later on. The roots of our understanding of architecture lie in our childhood, in our youth; they lie in our biography. Students have to learn to work consciously with their personal biographical experiences of architecture. Their allotted tasks are devised to set this process in motion.

We may wonder what it was that we liked about this house, this town, what it was that impressed and touched us—and why. What was the room like, the square, what did it really look like, what smell was in the air, what did my footsteps sound like in it, and my voice, how did the floor feel under my feet, the door handle in my hand, how did the light strike the façades, what was the shine on the walls like? Was there a feeling of narrowness or width, of intimacy or vastness?

Wooden floors like light membranes, heavy stone masses, soft textiles, polished granite, pliable leather, raw steel, polished mahogany, crystalline glass, soft asphalt warmed by the sun … the architect's materials, our materials. We know them all. And yet we do not know them. In order to design, to invent architecture, we must learn to handle them with awareness. This is research; this is the work of remembering.

Architecture is always concrete matter. Architecture is not abstract, but concrete. A plan, a project drawn on paper is not architecture but merely a more or less inadequate representation of architecture, comparable to sheet music. Music needs to be performed. Architecture needs to be executed. Then its body can come into being. And this body is always sensuous.

All design work starts from the premise of this physical, objective sensuousness of architecture, of its materials. To experience architecture in a concrete way means to touch, see, hear, and smell it. To discover and consciously work with these qualities—these are the themes of our teaching.

All the design work in the studio is done with materials. It always aims directly at concrete things, objects, installations made of real material (clay, stone, copper, steel, felt, cloth, wood, plaster, brick). There are no cardboard models. Actually, no "models" at all in the conventional sense, but concrete objects, three-dimensional works on a specific scale.

The drawing of scale plans also begins with the concrete object, thus reversing the order of "idea—plan—concrete object", which is standard practice in professional architecture. First the concrete objects are constructed; then they are drawn to scale.

We carry images of works of architecture by which we have been influenced around with us. We can re-invoke these images in our mind's eye and re-examine them. But this does not yet make a new design, new architecture. Every design needs new images. Our "old" images can only help us to find new ones.

Thinking in images when designing is always directed towards the whole. By its very nature, the image is always the whole of the imagined reality: wall and floor, ceiling and materials, the moods of light and color of a room, for example. And we also see all the details of the transitions from the floor to the wall and from the wall to the window, as if we were watching a film.

Often however, they are not simply there, these visual elements of the image, when we start on a design and try to form an image of the desired object. At the beginning of the design process, the image is usually incomplete. So we try repeatedly to re-articulate and clarify our theme, to add the missing parts to our imagined picture. Or, to put it another way: we design. The concrete, sensuous quality of our inner image helps us here. It helps us not to get lost in arid, abstract theoretical assumptions; it helps us not to lose track of the concrete qualities of architecture. It helps us not to fall in love with the graphic quality of our drawings and to confuse it with real architectural quality.

Producing inner images is a natural process common to everyone. It is part of thinking. Associative, wild, free, ordered, and systematic

thinking in images, in architectural, spatial, colorful, and sensuous pictures—this is my favorite definition of design.

Does Beauty Have a Form?

Apricot trees exist, ferns exist, and blackberries, too. But beauty? Is beauty a concrete property of a thing or an object that can be described or named, or is it a state of mind, a human sensation? Is beauty a special feeling inspired by our perception of a special form, shape, or design? What is the nature of a thing that sparks a sensation of beauty, that gives us a feeling at a certain moment of experiencing beauty, of seeing beauty? Does beauty have a form?

1 Music interrupts my writing. Peter Conradin is listening to a Charles Mingus recording of the 50s. A particular passage has caught my attention, a passage of great intensity and freedom in the calm, almost earthy sweep of its slow rhythm. In the pulse of that rhythm, the tenor saxophone speaks in warm and rough and leisurely tones that I almost understand—word by word. Booker Erwin, the sound of his horn hard and compressed, shrill but not brittle, porous despite the density; dry pizzicatos in Mingus's bass; no erotic, greasy "groove" that seeks to disarm and conquer. The music, thus heard, might give the impression of sounding stiff. But it isn't. It's wonderful. Incredibly beautiful, my son and I say, almost in unison, as we look at each other. I listen. The music draws me in. It is a space. Colorful and sensual, with depth and movement. I am inside it. For a moment, nothing else exists.

2 A painting by Rothko, vibrant fields of color, pure abstraction. To me it's only a question of seeing, a purely visual experience, she says. Other sensual impressions like smell or sound, materials or the sense of touch don't play a role. You enter the picture you're looking at. The process has something to do with concentration and meditation. It is like meditation, but not with an empty mind. You're fully alert and aware. Concentration on the picture sets you free, she says. You reach another level of perception.

3 The intensity of a brief experience, the feeling of being utterly suspended in time, beyond past and future—this belongs to many, perhaps even to all sensations of beauty. Something that has the radiation of beauty strikes a chord in me, and later, when it is over, I say: I was completely at one with myself and the world, at first holding my breath for a brief moment, then utterly absorbed and immersed, filled with wonder, feeling the vibrations, effortlessly excited and calm as well, enthralled by the magic of the appearance that has struck me. Feelings of joy. Happiness. The countenance of a sleeping child, unaware of being watched. Serene, undisturbed beauty. Nothing is mediated. Everything is itself. The flow of time has been halted, experience crystallized into an image whose beauty seems to indicate depth. While the feeling lasts, I have an inkling of the essence of things, of their most universal properties. I now suspect that these lie beyond any categories of thought.

4 The Renaissance theater in Vicenza. Steep rows. The wood worn and aged, great intimacy. A powerful sense of space, intensity. Everything is right, she says, so amazing, so natural, like a hand.

And later, the villa on the hill: She walks through the countryside and suddenly sees a jewel that takes her breath away. The building is radiant. As if it belonged to the landscape and the landscape belonged to it.

5 The beauty of nature touches us as something great that goes beyond us. Man comes from nature and returns to it. An inkling of the measure of human life within the immensity of nature wells up inside us when we come upon the beauty of a landscape that has not been domesticated and carved down to human scale. We feel sheltered, humble and proud at once. We are in nature, in this immeasurable form that we will never understand and now, in a moment of heightened experience, no longer need to because we sense that we ourselves are part of it.

I look out into the landscape; I gaze at the sea on the horizon, look at the masses of water; I walk across the fields to the acacias; I look at the elder blossoms, at the juniper tree and become still.

She is bathing in the Sicilian sea and dives under water. Her heart misses a beat. A huge fish passes close by, silent and infinitely slow. Its movements are untroubled and powerful and elegant. They have the self-evidence of millennia.

6 She loves beautiful shoes. She admires the craftsmanship, the material and above all their shape, their lines. She likes looking at shoes, not when people wear them but as objects whose shape is strictly defined by use and whose beauty transcends practical demands until they come full circle and say to her: "Use me, wear me." The beauty of a utilitarian object is the highest form of beauty, she adds.

7 As long as I can remember, I have always experienced the beauty of an artifact, an object created by man as a special presence of form, as a self-evident and self-confident hereness that is intrinsic to the object. Sometimes when such an object asserts itself in nature, I see beauty. The building, city, house, or street seems consciously placed. It generates a place. Where it stands, there is a back and a front, there is a left and a right, there is closeness and distance, an inside and outside, there are forms that focus and condense or modify the landscape. The result is an environment.

The object and its environment: a consonance of nature and artificially created work that is different from the pure beauty of nature—and different from the pure beauty of an object. Architecture, the mother of the arts?

8 She is standing with a group of younger people, mostly architects. It's drizzling; the air is warm. The men and women are standing in the courtyard of a villa. Their open umbrellas and sweeping, unbuttoned raincoats lend them an air of cosmopolitan elegance. The daylight around the group is mild. Light from above shines through a soft gray ceiling of clouds that could be interpreted as a thick layer of fog. It transforms the minute raindrops into particles of light. The landscape is filled with gentle radiance.

The faces of the men and women standing there seem serene. With unhurried, almost casual nonchalance, they take in the stately manor, the courtyard, the outhouses, the open wings of the wrought-iron gate. Occasionally someone glances at the hilly countryside. Mist rises. The cobblestones in the courtyard, the leaves on the trees, the grasses on the meadow glisten. The meandering gaze seeks the way to the Villa Rotonda of Andrea Palladio, which is supposed to be nearby. The scene has become a lasting image in her memory. She has written about it.

9 I remember the experience of houses, villages, cities, and landscapes, about which I now say they lent me an impression of beauty. Did these situations also seem beautiful to me at the time? I think so, but I'm not quite sure. The impression came first, I suppose, and reflection followed. And I know that certain things were not invested with beauty until afterwards, through subsequent impulses, conversations with friends, or conscious exploration of my still aesthetically unclassified recollections. I can also respond to beauty that others have experienced. I assimilate the impression it has made on them if I am able to create an image in my mind of the beauty others tell me about.

Beauty always appears to me in settings, in clearly delimited pieces of reality, object-like or in the manner of a still life or like a self-contained scene, composed to perfection without the least trace of effort or artificiality. Everything is as it should be; everything is in its place. Nothing jars, no overstated arrangement, no critique, no accusation, no alien intentions; no commentary, no meaning. The experience is unintentional. What I see is the thing itself. It captivates me. The picture that I see has the effect of a composition that appears extremely natural to me and at the same time extremely artful in its naturalness.

10 She turns the corner of a small shed and sees the new building for the first time. She comes to a halt, astonished, electrified. Something about the way the pillared building is standing there, the way it is made of porous stone and glass and fine-ringed wood and the way it forms a large courtyard with its older neighbors—the new body set down with non-geometrical precision in the balance of the masses and materials of the place—imparts feelings of attraction and aura, of energy and presence. It seemed as if everything I saw was in a state of balanced suspension. And the body of the new building seemed to vibrate, she said.

11 He is standing in the portal of San Andrea in Mantua. A tall portico of light and shadow, single rays of sun on the pilasters. A world of its own, no longer city but not yet the interior of the church. Pigeons are flying high up in shadowy regions where the carved figures and moldings fade out of sight. I hear but do not see them. Darkness abounds. The light that penetrates reveals fine particles of dust in the air. The air is thick, almost tactile. It seems as if the things under the portico in which I am standing, things more sensed than seen, have energized each other, as if they were in a unique state of mutuality, he says.

12 Our perception is visceral. Reason plays a secondary role. I think we immediately recognize beauty that is a product of our culture and corresponds to our education. We see a form framed and condensed into an emblem, a shape or a design, which touches us, which has the quality of being a great deal and possibly everything in one: self-evident, profound, mysterious, stimulating, exciting, suspenseful...
Whether the appearance that touches me really is beautiful cannot be properly judged by the form itself because the depth of feeling that belongs to the sensation of beauty is not ignited by the form as such but rather by the spark that jumps from it to me.

But beauty exists—although it makes relatively rare appearances and frequently in unexpected places. While in other places where we would expect it, it fails to appear.

Can beauty be designed and made? What are the rules that guarantee the beauty of our products? Knowing about counterpoint, harmonics, the theory of color, the Golden Section and "form follows function" is not enough. Methods and devices—all those wonderful instruments—are no substitute for content, nor do they guarantee the magic of a beautiful whole.

13 My task as a designer is difficult—by definition. It is related to artistry and achievement, intuition and craftsmanship. But also to commitment, authenticity, and a deep interest in subject matter.

To achieve beauty I must be at one with myself, I must do my own thing and no other because the particular substance that recognizes beauty and can, with luck, create it lies within me. On the other hand, the things I want to create—table, house, bridge—must be allowed to come into their own. I believe every well-made thing has an inherently appropriate order that determines its form. This essence is what I want to discover and I therefore stick firmly to the matter at hand in the process of designing. I believe in an accuracy of outlook and a truth content in real, sensual experience, which are beyond abstract opinions or ideas.

What does this house want to become, as an object of use, as a physical body, its materials firmly constructed and joined, its shape molded into a form that serves life? I ask myself and ask some more. What does this house want to be for its location on the city lane, in the

suburbs, in the battered landscape, on the hill in front of a stand of beeches, with a flight path overhead, in the light of the lake, in the shade of the forest?

14 "Apricot trees exist, apricot trees exist / Ferns exist; and black-berries ..."

The beginning of this essay as well as the lines that follow are indebted to Inger Christensen, whose poem "Alphabet" begins with these lines; her poem builds on the infinitely increasing rhythm of the Fibonacci numbers, a condensation of words in which she secures the world and thereby releases particles that sparkle and irritate.

The June night exists. The June night exists ...
and no one
in this flying summer, no one understands that autumn exists,
the aftertaste and the afterthought,
too, only the dizzying series of this
restless ultra-sound exists and the jade ear of the
bat turned toward the ticking haze;
never has the earth's inclination been so splendid,
never the zinc-white nights so white ...

Beauty, I think as I read these lines, is at its most intense when it is born of absence. I find something missing, a compelling expression, an empathy, which instantly affects me when I experience beauty. Before the experience, I did not realize or perhaps no longer knew that I missed it, but now I am persuaded by knowledge renewed that I will always miss it. Longing. The experience of beauty makes me aware of absence. What I experience, what touches me, entails both joy and pain. Painful is the experience of absence and pure bliss the experience of a beautiful form that has been ignited by the feeling of absence. In the words of writer Martin Walser: "The more we miss something, the more beautiful may become that which we have to mobilize in order to endure absence."

The Magic of the Real

There is the magic of music. The sonata begins with the first descending melodic line of the viola, the piano sets in, and there it is already, the instantaneous presence of a distinct emotion; the atmosphere of sound that envelops and touches me, that puts me in a special mood.

There is the magic of painting and poetry, of words and images, there is the magic of radiant thoughts. And there is the magic of the real, of the physical, of substance, of the things around me that I see and touch, that I smell and hear. Sometimes, at certain moments, the magic conveyed by a specific architecture or landscape, a specific milieu, is suddenly there; it has materialized like the measured growth of the soul, unnoticed at first.

It is Maundy Thursday. I'm sitting in the long loggia of the cloth hall. Facing the panorama of the square, its row of buildings, its church and its monuments. My back to the wall of the café. Just the right amount of people. A flower market. In the sun. It's 11 a.m. The wall on the opposite side of the square lies in shadow, bathed in a pleasant bluish light. Wonderful sounds: conversations close by, footsteps on the flagstones of the square, the murmuring of the crowd (no cars, no engine noise), once in a while distant sounds of construction. Birds, black dots in flight, they look eager and cheerful, a fast and jagged pattern of lines in the air. The holidays have just begun and seem to have slowed down the walking pace of the people. Two nuns, happily gesticulating, make their way across the entire square; light-footed, their hoods blowing in the wind. Each carrying a plastic bag. The temperature is pleasantly invigorating and warm at once. I am sitting on a couch upholstered in pale, faded green velvet. The bronze statue on a high plinth on the square in front of me has its back to me and joins me in looking at the twin-spired church. The spires each have different pinnacles; they are identical when they start out at the bottom and become increasingly distinct toward the top. One is taller than the other and has a gold crown. Soon B. is going to appear to the right, walking toward me diagonally across the square.

At the time that I wrote these comments about the atmosphere of the square, I was utterly enchanted with everything I saw. Rereading my notes now I wonder what it was that moved me so much.

Everything! Everything—the things, the people, the quality of the air, the light, the noises, the sounds and the colors. Material presence, textures and shapes as well. Forms that I can understand. Configurations that I can try to read. Physiognomies that strike me as beautiful.

But apart from all the physical materials, apart from the things and the people, there was something else that touched me—was it something related to me alone, to my mood, my feelings, my expectations as I sat there watching and listening?

"Beauty is in the eye of the beholder"—this sentence comes to mind as I write. Does it mean that everything I experienced at the time was primarily the expression and the outflow of my state of mind, of the mood that I happened to be in at the moment? Did the experience ultimately have little to do with the square and its atmosphere?

In order to answer that question, I conduct a simple experiment: I dismiss the square from my mind and the moment I do so, a curious thing happens: the feelings evoked by the situation begin to fade and even threaten to disappear. Without the atmosphere of the square, I realize I would never have experienced those feelings. Now it comes back to me: there is an intimate relationship between our emotions and the things around us. That thought is related to my job as an architect. I work at the forms, the physiognomies, at the physical presence of the things that constitute the spaces in which we live. In my work, I contribute to the existing physical framework, to the atmosphere of places and spaces that kindle our emotions.

The magic of the real: that to me is the "alchemy" of transforming real substances into human sensations, of creating that special moment when matter, the substance and form of architectural space, can truly be emotionally appropriated or assimilated.

As an architect, I can construct workable holiday homes, commercial buildings, or airports; I can build flats with good floor plans at affordable prices; I can design theaters, art museums, or show rooms that make an impact; I can apply forms to my buildings that satisfy the need for innovation or novelty, status or lifestyle.

It is not easy to do those things. It takes work. And talent. And more work. But that alone is not enough to come up with compelling, successful architecture born of those special moments of personal architectural experience, and it makes me wonder: can I, as an architect, invest what I design with whatever it is that actually constitutes the essence of an architectural atmosphere? Can I create that unique feeling of intensity and mood, of presence, well-being, rightness and beauty? Is it possible to give concrete shape to that which defines the magic of the real at a specific moment, to the spell that it casts on my experience of it, conjuring a quality that I would never otherwise experience?

There are small and large, impressive and important buildings or complexes that dwarf me, that oppress me, that exclude or rebuff me. But there also buildings or ensembles of buildings, both small ones and monumental ones, that make me feel good, that make me look good, that give me a sense of dignity and freedom, that make me want to stay awhile and that I enjoy using.

These are the works I feel passion for.

So when I'm working, I keep reminding myself that my buildings are bodies and need to be built accordingly: as anatomy and skin, as mass and membrane, as fabric, shell, velvet, silk, and glossy steel.

I try to make sure that the materials are attuned to each other, that they radiate; I take a certain amount of oak and a different amount of *pietra serena* and add something to them: three grams of silver or a handle that turns or maybe surfaces of gleaming glass, so that every combination of materials yields a unique composition, becomes an original.

I listen to the sound of the space, to the way materials and surfaces respond to touching and tapping, and to the silence that is a prerequisite of hearing.

The temperature of rooms is very important to me, how cool they are, how refreshing, the chiaroscuro of warmth that caresses our bodies.

I love thinking about the personal things that people surround themselves with in order to work, in order to feel at home and for which I create room, space, and place.

I like the idea of arranging the inner structures of my buildings in sequences of rooms that guide us, take us places, but also let us go and seduce us. Architecture is the art of space and it is the art of time as well—between order and freedom, between following a path and discovering a path of our own, wandering, strolling, being seduced.

I give thought to careful and conscious staging of tension between inside and outside, public and intimate, and to thresholds, transitions, and borders.

And to the play of scale in architecture. My dedication to finding the right size of things is motivated by the desire to create degrees of intimacy, of closeness and distance. I love placing materials, surfaces, and edges, shiny and mat, in the light of the sun, and generating deep solids and gradations of shading and darkness for the magic of light falling on things. Until everything is right.

The Light in the Landscape

The light of the moon

The light of the moon is a quiet reflection, large, even, and mild. The light of the moon comes from far away. That makes it quiet. I imagine the shadows that things cast on the earth in the light of the moon imperceptibly seeking separation. Though I can't tell with my bare eyes. I'm too small or too close to make out the cosmic angle between the source of light and the things it illuminates on earth.

When I start studying light and shadow, the light and shadow of the moon, the light and shadow of the sun, the light and the shadows produced by the lamp in my living room, I acquire a sense of scale and dimension.

I have always wanted to write a book about light. I can think of nothing that reminds me more of eternity, says Andrzej Stasiuk in his book *Dukla*. Events or objects stop or disappear or collapse under their own weight and when I look at them and describe them, he says, it is only because they refract light, because they shape it and give it a form that we are capable of understanding.

The light that meets the earth from afar

I want to think about the artificial light in my buildings, in our cities and in our landscapes, and I catch myself forever returning, like a lover, to the object of my admiration: the light that meets the earth from afar, the untold numbers of bodies, structures, materials, liquids, surfaces, colors, and shapes that radiate in the light. The light that comes from outside the earth makes the air visible, I can see it. In the Upper Engadine in autumn, for example, where the skies are already southern but the air is fresh.

Seen from a great height

Seen from a great height, the artificial lights with which people illuminate the night have a soothing effect. We illuminate our buildings and streets, we illuminate our planet, ward off little pieces of darkness and create islands of light on which we can see ourselves and the things that we have accumulated around us.

Sensing, smelling, touching, tasting, dreaming in the dark—that's just not enough. We want to see. But how much light do people need in order to live? And how much darkness?

Is there a spiritual condition or a life condition so sensitive that tiny amounts of light would be enough to ensure a good life? Or, to go even further: Are there some things we can experience only in dark, shaded places, in the darkness of night?

Two hunters from San Bernardino, who spent a few days and nights in an uncivilized mountain valley, describe coming home at night and looking down on their illuminated village—the tunnel entrance, the gas station, the cars—and how the familiar village suddenly seemed polluted.

Tanizaki Jun'ichiro, the author of *In Praise of Shadows*, once decided to watch the full moon at the Ishiyama Temple, but changed his mind when he learned that they would play a recording of the *Moonlight Sonata* for the entertainment of the visitors and install artificial lights to illuminate the site.

The light of the sun

Myriad small dots of light: the stars in the sky, fireflies in the woods, the artificial lights of nightscapes on earth. Small objects of light that radiate or reflect. The glass beads in a chandelier, for example.

The light of the sun, the day, that reaches the surface of the earth from outer space, is big and strong and directed. It is one light.

Darkness lives in the earth

Recently, on a mountain hike, A. observed that the colors of the Alpine flowers along the path are still aglow for a little bit after twilight has fallen, as if the flowers had stored the light and now have to release it, she tells me.

Darkness lives in the earth. It rises up out of it and returns to it like a strong breath, I read in Andrzej Stasiuk's *Dukla*.

The older I get, the more intense is my interest in the various ways and forms in which light appears in nature. I am amazed, I learn from that, and I am aware that it is the light of the sun that illuminates the buildings I envision. I hold spaces, materials, textures, colors, surfaces, and shapes up to the light of the sun; I capture this light, reflect it, filter it, screen it off; I thin it out to create a luster in the right spot. Light as an agent, I'm familiar with it. But when I really start thinking about it, I understand hardly anything.

The light in the landscape

The Light in the Landscape. Friederike Mayröcker uses this image to title a text that seems extremely autobiographical to me. Its many shades and shadows keep breaking out and into the light as she piles up the material of her words layer upon layer, describing and creating inner and outer landscapes.

Personal landscapes. Images and landscapes of longing, mourning, tranquility, joy, loneliness, sanctuary, ugliness, the pretension of pride, seduction. In my memory they all have a light of their own.

Is it even possible to imagine things without light?

Tanizaki Jun'ichiro praises shadows. In the dark depths of the traditional Japanese home, where shadows crouch in all the corners, the gold of a lacquer painting gleams, and gentle light is diffused through translucent paper stretched over the delicate wooden frame of a sliding door so that one can hardly distinguish the source of the daylight that captures and reflects the objects so beautifully in the half light.

Jun'ichiro praises shadows. And shadows praise light.

Shadowless modernism

If I remember rightly, I have seen buildings of classical modernism that celebrate the light and the landscape. Richard Neutra's houses in California, for example. Shadows do not seem to loom large in these architectural compositions. But brightness does, light and air and the outdoor view, the sensation of living in the landscape, of having the landscape flow into or through the rooms inside—the landscape with all of its lights and shadows. Watching the sun set in these houses is a magnificent experience. Later, when the house is no longer illuminated from outside, it has to generate its own lighting, its own illuminated atmosphere. With human light.

Los Angeles by night

Seen from an approaching aircraft that is gradually losing altitude, the nighttime illumination of Los Angeles looks like a magical image. Later, on the streets of the city, that same light seems pallid and sickly to me, an unnatural brightness in which the green lawns and bushes in the front yards of the houses look as if they were made of plastic.

Between sunset and sunrise

Between sunset and sunrise, we furnish ourselves with illumination of our own making, lights that we can switch on at will. These lights cannot be compared to daylight; they are too weak and too breathless with their flickering intensities and swiftly spreading shadows.

But when I do not think of these lights that we make ourselves as an attempt to eliminate darkness, when I think of them as night-time lights, as accentuated night, as intimate illuminated clearings that we carve out of the darkness, then they can become beautiful, then they can have a magic all their own.

Which lights do we want to switch on between sunset and sunrise? What do we want to illuminate in our buildings, cities, and landscapes? How and for how long?

Architecture and Landscape

I am happy to have the opportunity to talk about a few ideas that have been on my mind regarding the subject of architecture and landscape. What do I feel when I experience landscape? I look at Romantic artist Caspar David Friedrich's painting *Monk by the Sea*. An aesthetic experience: I see a man looking at the horizon line of the ocean with his back to the painter. Like the painter and the man in the painting, I look at the landscape, at the painted horizon, and feel the grandeur and vastness. A certain melancholy comes to the fore, imbued with the sense of a world that is infinitely bigger than I am but that offers me sanctuary. In addition to the feeling that nature is close to me and yet larger than I am, landscape also gives me the feeling of being at home. The sky, the smells, the lighting, the colors and shapes—the landscape of my childhood has become part of my flesh and blood and when I return to it, I am coming home. Landscape also contains history. People have always lived in landscapes and worked in landscapes. Sometimes the landscape suffers from having us live and work in it. Nonetheless, for better or for worse, it is there that the history of our involvement with the earth is stored. And that is probably why we call it a cultural landscape. So, along with the feeling that I am part of nature, the landscape also gives me the sense of being connected to history.

Where does this depth of feeling that we all associate with landscapes come from? I think there are special moments when we, as human beings, truly realize that we belong to living nature, that we come from it and that we will return to it. Experiencing landscapes seems to encourage transcendental thoughts of this kind. In contrast, cities strike me more as being about the here and now, and about people. Cities are the work of human beings. They bring people together; they foster exchange. In cities I am especially aware of the human space, all the housing, cult spaces, spaces for work, trade, politics, power and pleasure, accumulated in great quantity, intimate and public, sometimes invisible and yet present. I'm aware of the density a city has, for instance London, which figures in Edgar Allan Poe's tale, *The Man of the Crowd*, where he describes a particular flaneur whose great curiosity and fascination make him follow the trail of the city's energy, its life, its secrets. Like landscapes, cities are, of course, also repositories of history. But the experience of it is different.

I would describe the distinction between city and landscape like this: cities tend to excite and agitate me; they make me feel big or small, self-confident, proud, curious, excited, tense, annoyed … or they intimidate me. But the landscape, if I give it the chance, offers me freedom and serenity. Nature has a different sense of time. Time is big in the landscape while in the city it is condensed, just like the city's space.

In connection with landscape I think of the term beauty as well, because of my Romantic gaze. I have no agricultural access to the landscape; I do not see it as a means of production but experience it above all in sensual and aesthetic terms. And my perception of it changes depending on whether it is a natural landscape or a cultural landscape. To me, a purely natural landscape high up in the mountains, for example, is basically always beautiful. Even when nature's landscapes are harsh, rugged, aloof or barren and even when they frighten me, they never strike me as ugly. Immanuel Kant says: "In nature we are directly touched by godliness." My father, a mountain climber who never read Kant, said the same thing.

But as a rule we are surrounded by cultural landscapes. And when I envision traditional cultural landscapes where the earth is treated with care and wisdom, I see in them a beautiful union of human work and nature. I am not only thinking of the Alpine regions. The miles and miles of perfectly circular irrigation systems for the fields outside of Los Angeles appeal to me just as much. And major earthmoving projects like canals, dams and terraces, clearings, clear-cuts and reforestation also exert a strong aesthetic appeal—and I ask myself why. Speaking about the harmony between man and nature is hackneyed but it evidently does describe a specific condition: where the work of human beings takes care of nature, of the soil, the plants, the animals, I get a sense of how human beings depend on the earth and at the same time I begin to realize that this must be the source of the impression of beauty that I associate with my experience of landscape.

In addition to traditional cultural landscapes, there are other more recent ones in which I see no beauty at all. I think that is often related to the fact that the built objects of these modern cultural landscapes are not invested with an intrinsic value of their own and do not enter into a relationship with the landscape. Structures of this kind just seem to mushroom, to cover the landscape until it disappears. And it is extremely difficult for me to bear that loss. Urban sprawl for me is an expression of loss, the loss of landscape.

At this point, of course, I would theoretically have to argue: This is where a city emerges. It is simply about the first generation of buildings in a future urban conglomerate. Be patient and maybe in one or two hundred years, this agglomeration will be as fascinating as Los Angeles. And the young architects who have been trained in the world's metropolises will invent astonishing solutions for these new agglomerations. Not everything can be beautiful to begin with. But as far as I'm concerned this intermediate stage is the most desolate relationship between landscape and city that I can possibly imagine. Urban sprawl makes landscape disappear, and the more landscape that is taken away from me the more I suffer from the loss of beauty. I could only be reconciled if this process were ultimately to spawn the vital energy of a new city.

If I as a designer want to do justice to the landscape I am working in, I have to take three things into account. First I have to look hard at the landscape, at the woods and trees, the leaves, the grasses, the animated surface of the earth, and then develop a feeling of love for what I see—because we don't hurt what we love. We treat what we love as well as we possibly can. Secondly, I have to take care. That is something I have learned from traditional agriculture, which uses the soil but is, at the same time, sustainable. It takes care of the things that nourish us. Thirdly, I must try to find the right measure, the right quantity, the right size and the right shape for the desired object in its beloved surroundings. The outcome is attunement, harmony or possibly even tension. I think loving the landscape, looking at it with one's heart, is requisite to finding the right measure.

But how do I find the right measure? I venture to claim that we all immediately sense if the relationship between the building and the landscape in which it has been placed is disrupted, if the landscape is not enriched through the architectural intervention but simply threatens to disappear. Besides, this kind of sensing is not a theoretical task; first and foremost, it means having faith in sensual perception. For that reason, I as a designer have to go through the same procedure every single time: to look and really see, to admit love, to take care, to find the right measure and to envision the placement of the proposed building in the landscape over and over again in order to see if the landscape accepts it. I must strive to sense the measure of the landscape again and again. Through inner appreciation, not through theoretical argumentation.

So, in conclusion, I want to talk about the preferences, passions and sensations that motivate me when putting up a building in a landscape. First of all, I have to love the earth and the topography. I love the movement of the landscape, the flow and the structure of its forms; I try to imagine how thick the humus is; I see the hard bump in the meadow and sense the big boulder underneath and all the other things I don't know very much about, but that give me a wonderful feeling. When I plan my buildings, it is vital to me to take care of this surface. Even if I have to modify the topography, it should look as if it was always that way.

And when I build something in the landscape, it is important to me to make sure my building materials match the historically grown substance of the landscape. The physical substance of what is built has to resonate with the physical substance of the area. I observe in myself a conspicuous sensitivity to the relationship of place, material and construction. Material and construction have to relate to the place, and sometimes even come from it. Otherwise I have the feeling that the landscape does not accept the new building. For example, if a house with external wall insulation and a synthetic topcoat is placed in the landscape, it hurts me to see how shabby the surfaces look in the light of the sun. I am compelled to make a choice of material that ensures integrity and authenticity. Buildings in the landscape have to be able to age beautifully.

And without a delight in topography and the synthesis of materials, there is no form: I love precise and clear-cut form. Unclear and imprecise buildings look bad in the landscape. I note that time and again. Ugly, loveless artefacts instantly stick out in the landscape. So when I design something for a landscape, I make a clear typological choice. I try to design simple and clear anatomies and bodies that look self-evident. Essential interventions that are instantly comprehensible.

In conclusion a few remarks on the fusion of architecture and landscape. Well-placed objects never cease to enchant me. I think of buildings that stand in the landscape like sculptures and yet also seem to grow out of it. For example, driving along the Eisack Valley in South Tyrol makes me deliciously happy because I see beautiful self-contained objects everywhere: a monastery, a village, a castle, a little shed on a meadow. I love how sharp and pointed these small and large monuments are. And even when they are gigantic, like fortresses on their cliffs, they do not disturb the landscape, they celebrate it.

How they manage to do that seems to be their secret. But there is one thing that strikes me: many of these architectural objects that fuse with the landscape make a powerful or at least a distinctive impression. Basically a large object—a church, a castle, a compact village, a dam— always looks comparably small in a mountain landscape. It doesn't outshine its surroundings; it brings out the grandeur of the landscape. I can imagine that it is still possible today for someone to place a substantial piece of architecture in the Alps in the right place with the right content that would make the landscape resonate. Admittedly, designers who want to do that, and can, are a rarity. And clients who have faith in such designers may be an even greater rarity. Nonetheless, the path to follow is obvious: I must try to let an appreciation of the landscape swell inside me if I want to create a new place of concentration that yields a new up and down, a new left and right, a new front and back. New landmarks. Sometimes the synthesis succeeds: structure and landscape fuse, grow together and establish an inimitable place. The aura of such places means home.

The Leis Houses

Annalisa had always dreamed of living in a house built of wood. Whenever she talked to me about it, I had the impression of a cozy home in the mountains where she would live alone. The two of us as a couple or a family with children never came up in all the different versions that she described during the many years that we have lived together. It was obvious that she was describing a very personal feeling of home and hominess. She envisioned rooms out of wood and painted in various colors. Was she talking about the way Swiss mountain pine smells, about a crackling fire in the living room stove, about the special warmth of wood as a shell for the human body, the way she did recently? I don't recall exactly what she said but I still have the impression that there was something special emanating from the house that she described, something that applies only to houses made of solid timber, and not out of slats and boards and not out of plywood or veneers.

And now the house has been built. Light and bright, in the hamlet of Leis with its age-blackened wooden buildings at an altitude of 1500 m. We put up another new building next to it at the same time, a smaller sibling, two houses from the same family, the Leis houses. Last year all summer long, it seems to me, you could hear the carpenters hammering, sometimes in concert with the sound of farm machinery, the tinkling bells of goats grazing further up the slope and the bright sound of the church bells chiming in the bellcote of the lime-white St. Jacob's Chapel nearby. Legs wide apart, faces intent with concentration, but breaking into a smile if one caught their eye, the young men stood on the walls, hammering down the beams with their sledgehammers,

usually working in pairs to a rhythmical beat. Swinging their hammers overhead, they slammed down the beams until the double tongue was flush in the double groove of the beam below, the beams tightly placed and assembled to form a wall.

Smoothly planed solid timbers, 11 cm wide, 20 cm high and up to 6.60 m long, were stacked on top of each other, layer upon layer, forming walls three stories high, the corners connected using the ancient and elegant dovetail joint or, if the interior layout was such that the corners had to be flush, with classical finger joints.

Wall beams, ceiling beams, roof beams, window frames of wood, connectors of metal, steel dowels, special extra long screws, wall ties, slotted plates, tension cables—these components all arrived pre-processed at the construction site; the solid timbers, precision cut to size, were tied together and plastic wrapped in large bundles for transport to ensure that, until use, the oven-dried timber retained the proper humidity as defined by the engineers: fourteen percent for the inside walls and seventeen percent for the façades. Every hole, every mortise, every tenon, every notch, dovetail or ledge was already in the right beam in the right place. Some 5000 beams for the two houses, hardly any two alike. Constructing meant assembling.

Before arriving at the construction site, the beams are milled in a fully automated joinery machine in the workshop of the timber construction company. Standing behind glass, we watch the fluid, staccato work of the machine. Having already been planed on four sides and milled with double tongue and double groove in another machine, the timber is precisely tracked with powerful pressure rollers for processing from left to right through the approximately man-sized metal cabin of the automated machine. Saws, drill bits and routers rise and fall, move forwards and backwards. The tools are sharp. The precision is great.

In order to cut the wood to size in the workshop before transporting it to the construction site and building the houses, the timber company's engineer wrote digital instructions for the computerized machine, using the data from the construction plans that our architects had generated on the computer after the design phase had been completed.

Our Leis houses have big windows. They extend from wall to wall and from floor to ceiling. They frame the landscape and welcome its images inside the house.

The traditional construction of log cabins, consisting of four walls that form a boxlike unit, does not permit large windows, as making large holes in the walls of the boxes would undercut their stability.

The plan of the Leis houses shows a number of small, traditionally constructed boxes in different sizes and shapes for the utility rooms, the stairs, the pantries, toilets and baths. These small rooms are freestanding units in the ground plan and are horizontally linked by the ceilings of the stories. Hence, the ceilings and utility rooms form the load-bearing structure of the buildings. The glazed spaces between the utility rooms create large panorama windows. The side walls of two utility rooms standing opposite reach out towards the view and, along with the floors and ceilings of laminated timber in between, they form wide bay windows to live in.

In the course of working on the Leis houses, we managed to wrest quite a bit from the principles of the traditionally constructed wooden box. To begin with, we converted the wooden box—the main living

room in the Alpine farmhouses in our area—into a smaller utility room. Then we placed these rooms in the ground plan as pillars, layered above each other in section and interconnected from story to story with wide laminated ceiling panels. The exposed ends of the walls are held together, where necessary, with steel pins or cables.

In this way, the two buildings are spacious and filled with light; the design also allowed for an expansive layout of rooms that open and close. Walking through the house means moving from view to view. The presence of the solid timber is tangible everywhere, intimate and close to the body; gentle, silky and shiny, it radiates in the light.

The houses are now slowly drying out and the wood is shrinking. The stories will lose a little bit of height in the next few years: about two or three centimeters. But our windows, doors and stairs, the pipes for the plumbing and the built-in closets, all fixed in place as they should be, are prepared for the wood that contains them to continue moving.

A Way of Looking at Things

Lecture written November 1988, SCI-ARC Southern California Institute of Architecture, Santa Monica

The Hard Core of Beauty

Lecture written December 1991, Symposium Piran, Slovenia

From a Passion for Things to the Things Themselves

Lecture written August 1994, Alvar Aalto Symposium, "Architecture of the Essential," Jyväskylä, Finland

The Body of Architecture

Lecture written October 1996, Symposium "Form Follows Anything," Stockholm, Sweden

Teaching Architecture, Learning Architecture

Written September 1996, Accademia di architettura, Mendrisio, Switzerland

Does Beauty Have a Form?

Slightly revised version of a lecture on "Venustas," given at the Department of Architecture of the Federal Institute of Technology, Zurich, November 1998
The quoted passages are from the poem "Alphabet" in: Inger Christensen, *Ein chemisches Gedicht zu Ehren der Erde, Auswahl ohne Anfang ohne Ende*, edited by Peter Waterhouse (Salzburg and Vienna: Residenz Verlag, 1997)

The Magic of the Real

Lectio Doctoralis delivered 10 December 2003 on the occasion of the Laurea Honoris Causa in Architettura award of the Università degli Studi di Ferrara, Facoltà di Architettura

The Light in the Landscape

Lecture written in the framework of the Swiss National Research Project "Fiat Lux" for a reading at the Bar Falena, Chiasso, Switzerland, 13 August 2004

Architecture and Landscape

Unscripted lecture given at the conference "Bauen in der Landschaft" in Bolzano, 25 February 2005

The Leis Houses

Essay written for: Diego Giovanoli, *Facevano case* (Malans / Chur: Pro Grigioni Italiano, 2009) pp. 390–392

Peter Zumthor

Born in Basel in 1943, trained as a cabinetmaker at the shop of his father, as a designer at the Kunstgewerbeschule Basel and as an architect at Pratt Institute, New York. In 1979 established his own practice in Haldenstein, Switzerland.

Selected buildings: *Protective Housing for Roman Archaeological Excavations,* Chur, Switzerland, 1986; *Sogn Benedetg Chapel,* Sumvitg, Switzerland, 1988; *Homes for Senior Citizens,* Chur, Masans, Switzerland, 1993; *Therme Vals,* Switzerland, 1996; *Kunsthaus Bregenz,* Austria, 1997; *Swiss Sound Box, Swiss Pavilion, Expo 2000 Hannover,* Germany, 2000; *Documentation Center "Topography of Terror,"* Berlin, Germany, constructed parts of 1997 demolished in 2004 by Berlin State; *Kolumba Art Museum,* Cologne, Germany, 2007; *Bruder Klaus Field Chapel,* Wachendorf, Germany, 2007; *log houses for Annalisa and Peter Zumthor, Unterhus and Oberhus,* Vals, Leis, Switzerland, 2009.

© Photographs: Laura J. Padgett, Frankfurt / Main,
taken in the Zumthor residence, July 2005

Layout and Cover: Hannele Grönlund, Helsinki

© Texts: Peter Zumthor, Haldenstein

Translation: Maureen Oberli-Turner (essays 1988–1996),
Catherine Schelbert (essays 1998–2009)

Library of Congress Cataloging-in-Publication data
A CIP catalog record for this book has been applied for at the Library of Congress.

Bibliographic information published by the German National Library
The German National Library lists this publication in the Deutsche Nationalbibliografie;
detailed bibliographic data are available on the Internet at http://dnb.dnb.de.

This book is also available in a German (ISBN 978-3-0346-0555-7) and a French language
edition (ISBN 978-3-0346-0582-3).

First edition 1998, Lars Müller Publishers, Baden, Switzerland.
Reprint 1999 and second, expanded edition 2006,
Birkhäuser Verlag, Basel, Switzerland.

Revised Reprint 2017 of the third, revised edition
© 2010 Birkhäuser Verlag GmbH, Basel
P. O. Box 44, 4009 Basel, Switzerland
Part of Walter de Gruyter GmbH, Berlin / Boston

Printed on acid-free paper produced from chlorine-free pulp. TCF ∞

Printed in Germany

ISBN 978-3-0346-0585-4

9 8 7 6 5 4

www.birkhauser.com